Where All Is Brought To Light

Where All Is Brought To Light

Poems

Heather Anderson Grant

Printed in the United States of America
First printing, 2023

Cover Artwork by Ellen MacDonald
Book Design by Wanji Lee

Author's Photo: Lifetouch
Typeface: Garamond

Library of Congress Control Number: 2023934551

Summary: A collection of poems of the poet's observations,
conversations, and mystical experiences
in and with the natural world.

ISBN 979-8-218-95119-1

www.heatheragrant.com

For the Natural World
with its fierce and exquisite beauty

ACKNOWLEDGMENTS

I wish to thank the editors of the following publications in which these poems, sometimes in slightly different form, first appeared.

Blueline: "Walk in the Woods"
Bulletin of the American Dahlia Society: "Dahlias in October"
Hawai'i Pacific Review: "After Tides"
Loose Hair Press: "Rainy Season," "Geogony"
Main Street Rag: Voices from the Porch: "Out of the Fog"
Spillway: "Milking the Lavender"
The Word Works: Whose Woods These Are: "Rising Moon"

Contents

Leaves and Wings

Before Crossing

Light in the Shadows

Where All Is Brought To Light

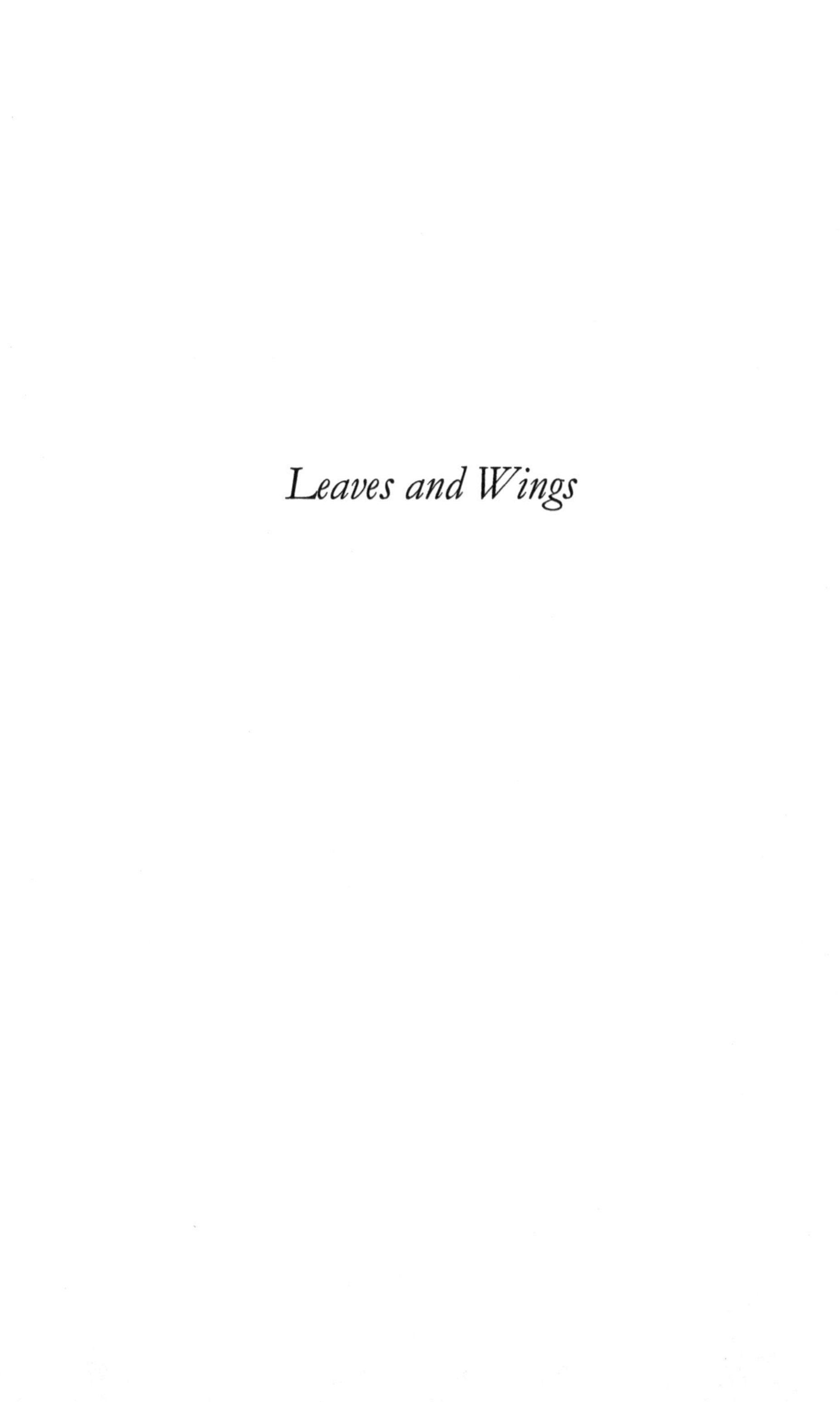
Leaves and Wings

Out of the Fog

After heavy late winter snows, warm winds
blow up from the south, lifting white clouds
from snowbanks piled high
along walkways, parking lots, streets,
fog so thick it seems the sky has lowered
and we are lifted into it, quieted, expectant
as a sheet of paper or blank canvas

We sit on the verandah with earth-filled pots,
fog on the other side of the railing.
I haltingly say, *I am on the edge of new words,*
and at once a flock of small dark birds appears
out of the fog flying straight toward us,
black marks against all that whiteness,
swings up and over the roof,
then gone

Spring Arrives

Light through tiny drifting
snowflakes,

magnolia's green leaves reflect
noon sun, wind rustles

through birdless trees,
gnarled roots press up

through thawing earth.
Nearby tulip trees throw spindly shadows

across the lawn, their seed pods fuzzy
as pussy willows,

promise of fuchsia blossoms.
I walk to the edge of the lawn,

my eye drawn to the sixty-foot pine,
refuge of old crows,

look up into symmetrical branches,
feathery evergreen needles wavering

as short shadows and orange needles
circle its trunk.

Large roots rise above ground,
run far across the lawn,

holding fast.
A single crow glides

through changing air
to the top of the pine.

Morning suddenly silent.

Hyacinth

A pointed hat presses
through thawing earth,
the lavender eye peers
above the surface,
curious

April Tango

Afternoon winds tease a tall weeping cherry,
flowers lusciously pink, limbs loose
run through the wind's hair.

Spring's amorous heat chilled by midnight.
In the morning, the cherry is draped
with ermine snow.

A noon sun draws open the heavy coat,
snow drips from long limbs,
blossoms unruffled, deeply pink.

Once more the cherry sways in spring air.

Afire in Green

A blast of early heat,
and winter trees burst into leaf,
glowing chartreuse

At the edge of the woods,
we sit reverent before a gigantic oak,
green leaves flickering,
a luminescent aura floats beyond branches
into open air, lights up a dark purple sky,
brighter than a full moon rising above the meadow

Next day, the sky is yellow green,
green smoke flows over the land,
drapes trees diaphanous green,
the air swells, green ash settles.
I brush the dust off the porch table
and chairs before sitting down—
my fingers tingle and burn

Soon trees will draw fires
inside, green darken, desire
twisting, turning,
reaching for the sun

Violets

Late winter sky
sleepy bee flits
among wild violets

Fluttering Wings

Sparrows and finches jostle
in the jacaranda trees,
shake leaves, and dapple light
while I take my lunch
among fluttering
wings and leaves.

One afternoon, to frighten
a sparrow off the road,
I pressed down
on the gas pedal instead of the brake
then drove on,
hoping the sparrow had flown off.
The next day there was
silence in the trees.
For days and weeks I sat
on the hard stone benches,
the trees sprinkling light,
but never again birds.

Years later, my children
found a sparrow fallen
from its nest in the grass.
I cupped its small frame
and gave it light with my hand,
the tiny beating chest
grew quiet, then still.

Norfolk Island Pine

A branch caught,
snaps from the trunk
as we come through
the front door,
but not clean through,
phloem exposed.
I lift the branch,
wrap it with cotton strips,
cinching the wound.

Weeks pass,
spikey needles green
along the branch
not yet healed.
I wait for it
to brown,
make a final clip.

More weeks pass,
new growth sprouts
above the wound—
pine sap sealed
the tear.

Every winter
the pine drops
leaves, branches,
makes room
for growth
pushing up
from young
saplings below,

shape shifting
as the pine inches
toward the ceiling.

Night Rain

Sky tornado green,
thunder rumbles,
wind throws rain
through bending trees,
the newscast interrupted,
flash flood warnings,
lightning crackles,
a neighbor's dog yelps.

Streetlamps float
in the dark,
lights on
in long windows,
the building a Mondrian
in beige and grey.
Flashing red,
the radio tower
syncopates
with lightning.

Dark night,
soggy, swollen earth,
leaves dripping
rain lullabies
for dreamless sleep,
day into night
into day,
rain.

Echo

As she leaned against the kitchen counter,
my German grandmother sipped
her cup of black coffee,
considering tea sandwiches
for the German American book club.
As I brushed white crusts
from the cutting board
into the kitchen garbage,
she sighed,
You are not thinking of the birds.

At seven, I stood at the window
in the sunroom early mornings
watching Grandmother toss
breadcrumbs into the yard,
her worn hands reaching
as the birds scattered.

A generation later, we harvested
most of the collard greens and chard.
Overnight, birds nibbled the rest
right down to white stems.

Blue in May

Brilliant in an azure sky
the sun withdraws, pulling
a gray mantle over the landscape,
colors soften, and my eye turns
to the periwinkle at garden's edge,
blue haze of cornflowers
in an open field, dotted
with Queen Anne's lace,
indigo eye in the center.
From the corner of my eye,
a handsome man in a cerulean
blue sports car tosses his head,
cobalt candy wrapper pressed
against the newly tarred street,
purple-blue thistle
in cracked pavement,
a large turquoise ring
on a woman's gnarled hand,
and a young mother wearing
a blousy lapis top, earrings to match,
pushes a denim baby carriage,
her child in a blue shirt
turns and flashes a smile,
the kindness in his quiet
blue eyes draws me in

Cherry Blossoms

As squirrels munch cherry
blossoms, birds arrive and chirp,
Wait for the cherries!

Morning Glories

Mornings when my mind's
not still, thoughts fly out,
swirl around every distraction,
I look to morning glories
throwing themselves
across space,
anchoring to anything
vertical, twisting
in the opposite direction,
swaying in the breeze.

A long vine wraps itself
around a tomato stem,
and I gently unwind it,
curl the vine around
the metal railing.
Later, the vine has unwound,
reaches again for the tomato.
Unaware, a bumblebee sips
from purple trumpets.

Encounter

Geranium scent rises,
coral petals shower
onto warm brick.
Startled,
a hummingbird
flits inches
from my face,
his dark blue
head circled
in gold,
wings whirring.
He darts closer,
hovering—
we hold our gaze,
move closer, merging
in the starry night.

Among Sequoias

We walk respectfully
in a pantheon of giant,
magnanimous trees,
their vigor running up
hundreds of feet
straight into sky.
Sequoias, present
to our history,
live for thousands of years,
then simply fall.

*****

I rest my hands
on dark red bark,
feet thick, dense,
layered like skin,
press ear to trunk,
listen for the pulse,
then lean full body,
arms extended,
my feet resting
on pine needles,
and silky red silt.

*****

A wellspring flows
up and down my body
as the sun falls,
skirting the forest floor.

Wind Chime

I move at wind's will
among oak leaves,
a soft, melodic knocking
in a gentle southeast wind.

But when a Nor' easter
blows steady,
my string-held knocker
catches the wind,
wraps me in leafy branches.

I hang quietly
among dappled leaves
when the wind is still,
dream of years
when I was tall and green,
huddling in groves
of family bamboo,
pale leaves shooting out like fireworks.

Cricket Song

swings
between twilight
and unlit rooms,
filling the dark house
with summer

Milking the Lavender

Hidden among summer verdure, the elegant lavender,
frame still intact, silver branches, leaves cascading over the
pot, releases such sweet scent as I strip crinkled leaves from
stems, rub them between fingers, both hands in the pot as
far down as the roots, mixing roots and stems and leaves
until the earth is saturated, gather handfuls in my palms,
breathe lavender earth, rub it on my face, arms, hair until
washed up in lavender, innocent as a sleep-covered child

Swimming in the Rain

Rain drops softly
onto the surface
of the silent pool.
I dive into
stillness,
coasting underwater
until fingers break
the surface.

Water glides along
my body,
arm over arm,
breathe,
over arm over arm,
breathe,
up and back,
flip over,
arch back,
float like a lily
under a summer shower,
pearl drops
on my face.

The rain drums harder
onto the pool.
I pull myself out
moments
before thunder and
the terrifying flash.

Horse Bones

Bleached horse bones wash up on the beach,
bones from broken down bodies,
Arabian beauties that never made it

across the Atlantic to the new world.
Long leg bones unsplintered,
smaller bones scattered along the shore.

A man squints, and hundreds of ghosts canter
above the waves, then splash
in the shallows onto the beach.

With fire in his eyes, the tall dark horse
lowers its head, moist breath
on the man's ear, nudges him to grab

hold of the bristly mane, pull himself
up and over onto high haunches,
settle into the hollow of its back.

Horse and rider climb through surf
onto firm wet ground,
the man strokes the long silky neck, leans forward,

listens to the whinnies from farther down the beach,
his knees into the horse's belly; they canter
along the coastline into morning light.

California Burning

Summer lightning thrusts
into parched earth,
dried grasses
in the forests
tinder for a blaze.
The first tree catches
fire running up the trunk
along the ground
to the next pine,
and the next,
from crown to crown.

Wind drives hard
along mountain ridges,
sparks shower
from a crimson sky,
hillsides disappear.

Down mountain slopes
rivers race blood red,
blood orange,
tree skeletons shake,
towers of black smoke lift
above the slopes.

In the hellish flames,
screams of frantic animals
are not heard, birds fly
out of a searing wind.

Days later, ghostly trees
stand with pared-off limbs,

mountain slopes covered
in thick ash—
an eerie silence drifts
in neighborhoods still smoldering.

I hear Earth calling, *Sister, Sister*

Before Crossing

Changing Tides

Superstition Mountains, Arizona

Birds draw a line,
lift, rise higher,
slide down a wind slope
crossing an entire canyon,
coast to a low ledge before landing

The patterns never the same,
the wind shifts,
rolls in the opposite direction,
birds glide up and down canyon walls
riding the changing tide

Something in me flies up
to a hawk hovering high in the wind,
rises toward the sun,
down over the cottonwoods,
and out through the canyons

At Desert's Edge

Zenith sun
sears deep
into the body,
draws fear
to the surface
until it bursts
out of its skin

Shadows, secrets
tumble across the desert

The body purified, translucent

Desert Night

Phoenix, Arizona

Air heavy all day,
by night the sky pulses,
North Mountain unmasked
suddenly outlined in lavender

Lightning strikes repeatedly,
rain drives into earth
not more than dust,
releases grass and leaf perfume
into a cooling wind

The night fecund

Monsoon near Phoenix

Towers of red dust a mile high
roll across the land east to west,
dropping canyons of sand
onto the valley. Phoenix
burns at the horizon.
The city disappears
in a glow of pink fog,
lights blink in the buildings
downtown, the fire alarms go off,
and the city grows dark.
Further out, hot sand
blows against the houses,
comes through cracks
in the windows,
the palm trees twist and bend
in the red-orange sky,
curlicue lightning
almost comic.
A bitter odor lingers.

The thunderstorm passes—
a full double rainbow arcs over the valley.

Next morning, the air
is clean and brittlebush reappear
on the stony desert floor,
their yellow flowers glistening.

Evening Stroll

Sahuaro Ranch Park, Glendale, Arizona

Peacocks gather at dusk
after wandering all day
over coarse desert grass,
and spin in slow wide circles,
fanning blue and green-eyed feathers,
puff out blue iridescent chests
as they strut in solemn formation,
dragging long tails.

Their bashful mates
follow behind,
roll from side to side,
amble toward
the ironwood trees
behind the barn.

As they arrive
at the homestead,
the males cry out, flap
short wings, scramble
up ceramic tiles
to gabled rooftops,
each to his own perch,
preening as they posture
in blue silhouette
under the full moon.

Before Crossing

From the top of North Mountain,
the sun drops below the horizon,
a crescent moon rises
above the city's glow
as we sit in an outcropping
with mesquite and barrel cactus
before sliding our bodies flat
across metamorphic rock,
close our eyes

The wind billows over
and around us,
rhythmic as an incoming tide,
washes over rocks,
our ancient bodies,
before crossing inland seas

Whalebones

South Mountain, Phoenix, Arizona

The sun lowers,
shadows flow over large, rounded hills,
the valley rolls as an ocean swells
to mountains before a storm.
A whale plunges across the sky,
only his bones ripple in blue

Rainy Season

Honolulu, Hawaii

The rain starts tinny on the roof,
drips from banana and ti leaves,
drenches papayas and mangos,
pelts percussively
into red dirt
down to the first layers of roots,
then lets up—
for a moment the sky brightens

Curtains of rain
fall for hours,
day after day
after day.
The rain seeps down
through sedimentary,
metamorphic layers,
rivulets turn to streams
then rivers underground,
filling giant lakes,
overflowing

Hawaiian Blessing

Nudged awake at 3:00 a.m.
I stumble barefoot to thick, wet grass—

The eastern sky a dark purple tapa.
Misty rain falls on monkeypods,
now dark contours in the neighbor's yard,
while a swollen August moon hangs
low in a bright western sky
spotlighting trees.
A faint line begins to draw up
through the dense, rounded foliage,
curves high above trees over a bank of white clouds,
then, leading to the horizon
fans to a palette of seven.
Up through the same dark green, another line
draws an arc high above the first,
colors fade in again—
night rainbows

Tapa is a coarse cloth made in the Pacific islands from the pounded bark of the paper mulberry widely grown as a shade tree.

Before a Honolulu Sunset

Every evening my father strolled
along the Ala Wai canal before dinner.
Once during a visit, he leaned over
and whispered, *I have a surprise.*
Accompanied by the scent of pikake,
we walked along the Ala Wai
to a convenience store,
and sat down on a wooden bench
facing an ancient banyan tree
filled with hundreds of tiny island birds.
I began to talk, and he raised a finger to his lips,
The birds begin to sing just after 5:00

Returning home from errands
on a rainy fall evening,
our arms loaded down
with grocery bags and backpacks,
my children and I pause
and listen to the sweetest bird song
coming from tightly woven holly bushes.
As they rush to the door
to get out of the rain, I linger

*Pikake are small white flowers with a delicate fragrance similar to
gardenia and grow throughout Hawaii.*

Hibiscus

Red hibiscus holds
tight in the bud,
unfolds
before the heat of day—

Such ruby lusciousness

Sailing

Wahiawa, Hawaii

It is late evening, and I am in the garden
watching stars shoot across an August sky,
trade winds caressing my face and salty lips.

Somewhere in the South Pacific on a summer night
in August, two teenagers stood at the bow
of a cruise ship, leaning back against cool metal,
cheeks brushed by sultry trade winds,
engine steady, water lapping against the hull.
Letting go of my hand, he gently turned my face to his,
on salty lips, first kiss—

This kiss gone around the world
before it kissed my lips
again, this night
in the lush highlands of Oahu.

Transplant

Pearl City, Hawaii

She holds red beans carried
from the Mainland in her palm,
beans to be planted
in evenly spaced mounds,
when a neighbor,
perusing her garden, interrupts,

If you want more
tomato plants,
just snap off a branch,
dig a hole, pour in water,
cover the stem.
Roots will grow.

Dizzy from volcanic earth
saturated with island flowers,
she raises her head to her neighbor's voice
as fragrant trade winds blow wisps
of hair across her face

Collage

Sitting cross-legged on damp crabgrass
before a large pile of picked fruit,
my toddler son and I peel tangerine
after tangerine under the tree's canopy,
slurping sweet tart slices,
juice dripping, deliciously sticky,
eat until the pile is seeds and peels,
and we are gorged and content,
resting under a sky streaked pink and orange,
the trades blowing through clusters
of yellow and orange cosmos

After Tides

Grains of sand carried by tides
float into
the folds of my body
unforeseen
uninvited
they rub
tender flesh
raw

I turn events over
examine, review
and turn again
layer
upon
layer

Some days it hurts
as much
as first days of knowing

After many tides have come
gone
these grains are lifted

a strand of pearls
to offer
and wear

Drifting Blossoms

She dives through turquoise waves past the breakers,
the sea sparkles, washes over plumeria leis
as she drifts in a bower of blossoms,
cradled by the rocking ocean,
sweet plumeria and sea salt.

Thinking of her father,
she lifts the leis circling her neck,
offers the sunlit blossoms to the sea,
then turns, backstroking:
gentle waves carry her to shore.

That night, under starry Obon skies,
she places a paper lantern in the Ala Wai canal,
letting it drift out to the Pacific in a flotilla of thousands.

*Obon is a time of Japanese Buddhist observances held in summer
to express gratitude for loved ones who have passed on.*

Geogony

Underneath us
the earth arches, contracts

We float above
this new birth, wake

at distant meridians,
partner the other:

New constellations appear

Geogony is a science or theory of the formation of the earth.

Rising Moon

Rising moon
a teacup tipped
on the horizon
the sky pours out

Hold no regret
in parting

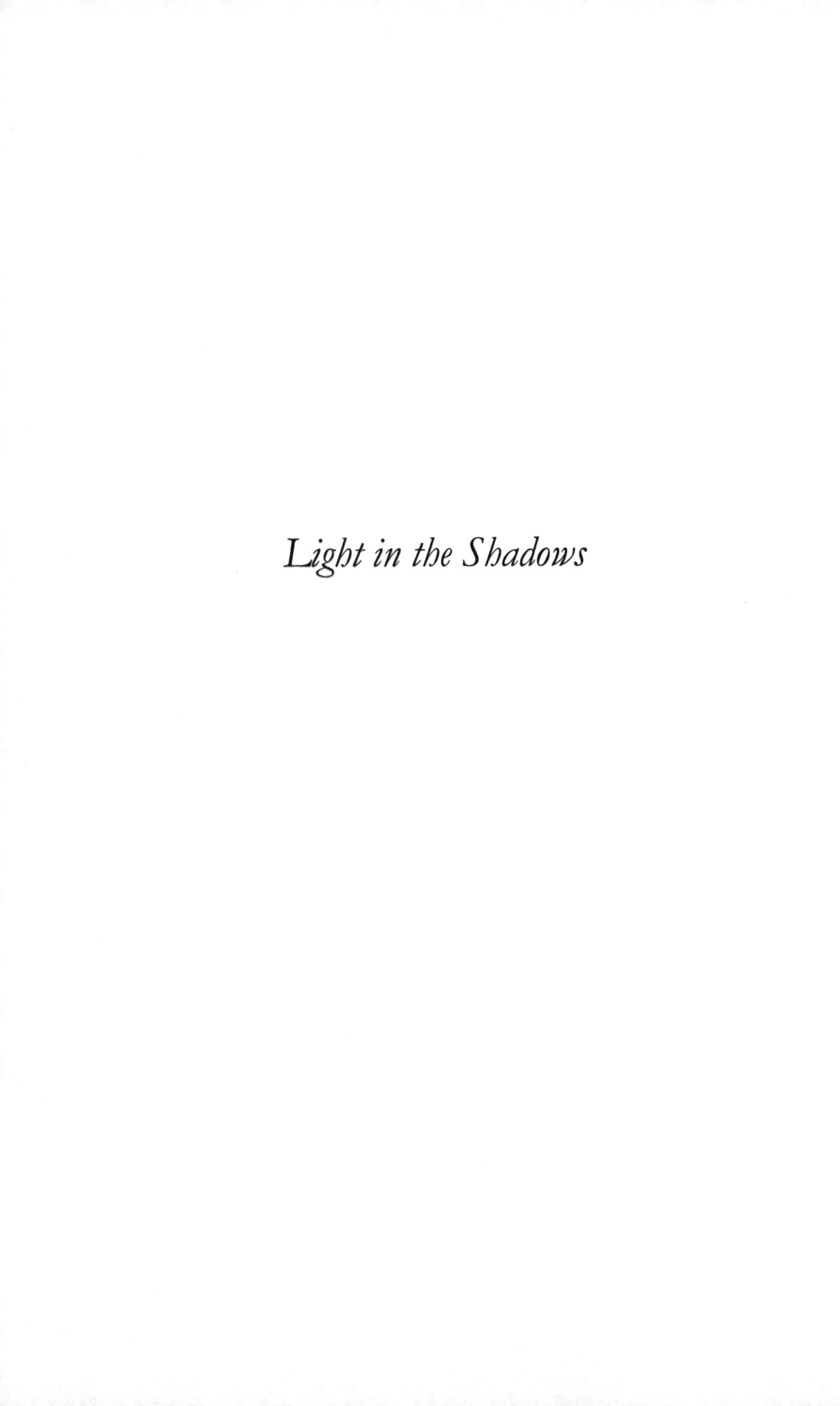

Light in the Shadows

Words Slip

The time of year when words slip from me,
gradually falling off until I am bare, stripped
as they flutter down inside, curl, become dormant,
waiting to emerge when light comes back.

Birds gather, fly south across a pale sky,
ride streams of invisible currents rolling up and down.
For miles and miles they fly unbroken lines,
their destination etched by repetition, ancestral longing.

Every year I lose words as leaves turn,
reach as they fall from my outstretched hand.

Impatiens

Shaking earth from annuals
into pots left on the verandah
to soak in winter light,
I snap off drooping stems
from the impatiens,
toss them in a brown bag
when at the very base
of stems,
new leaves and tiny flowers
begin at the joint
between light and dark,
fed by fall rain
and earth kept warm
by leaves after
first frost.

I place the impatiens
in a southern window
with lavender, mint, parsley.
Within days, pink flowers open,
acceptance arrives
on the scent of lavender.

On Cue

A flock of chattering starlings
hops on the branches of a large oak,
tumbles acorns on my head, hands, book
and the picnic table where I sit.
Unable to read, I open my notebook and write,
The starlings prepare to fly south.
Silence in the oak.
A rush of downward air as starlings lift,
fly out of sight

Dahlias in October

Frost approaches a forest of dahlias—
large, magnificent heirlooms
stand tall in the upper gardens,
smaller poms multi-colored fill in below,
bouquets of both fill rooms,
gifts to neighbors and friends

Blossoms reach for the October sun
knowing soon the chill will fell them,
heads nodding, drooping over leaves;
stems then cut just above the ground,
tuber roots wrapped, gently stored
in the basement
where they hunger to sleep,
to gather color and shape in dreams,
nesting against each other until late spring

Autumn Morning in Sperryville

Blue Ridge Mountains, Virginia

Morning sun warm on the long porch—
a sudden wind whooshes across the pines,
takes whatever I am thinking
into the woods

Early Autumn

Colored leaves rain
in the heavy winds,
swirl on the porch,
casting color across windows

A draft like inverse rain
lifts the leaves up—
and over the rooftops

Crows Fly

across a mottled sky
on a changing wind.

The darkness in me
flies straight out
with the crows.

Walnut Harvest

The summer hammock was strung inside the barn
to dry walnuts falling like black gold.

Handful by handful she tossed in walnuts
until the hammock sagged to the cement floor.

Black walnuts were her quick cash from the farmer's market
for walnut spread and walnut bread and walnut cakes.

There are some who prefer it simple—walnut meat
in the half shell—which she discovered early one morning

as she slid the heavy barn door open
to a sprung hammock, a line of broken shells

trailed to a knot hole, another gnawed in the canvas—
a perfect chute: walnut chasing walnut to the dusty floor.

From the kitchen window, she looks out to the yard,
watching fat gray squirrels high up in the empty walnut trees.

Conversation with the Moon

You often wake me
when full,
shining through
unshuttered windows,
insistent.
I finally rise.

This morning you woke me
at 4:00 a.m.,
and wanting to ignore your invitation,
I pulled the covers tight
when my husband, coffee in hand,
whispered through the door,
A lunar eclipse!

Floating mid-heaven,
your silver body glows,
Earth's shadow, a blue halo,
moves slowly across your radiance,
your waxing lunar phases
travel in fast slow motion
within the hour;
by dawn a tangerine globe shimmering,
whisper,

This is why I woke you

Silhouettes

Dark trees against purple sky,
fog swirls through
empty spaces,
gathers where trunk
and branches meet,
flows through the webbing of twigs

In the stillness,
old shadows lift

Late Autumn

The library quiet except
for the drone of radiators,
cold rain framed
by windows;
a red maple brushes
against the glass

After the rain,
crickets sing

Egret

The Potomac flat like black glass
a snowy egret flies just above the surface
straight as a slow-moving arrow

Wild Winds

race down from the north.
We rush back inside.
Our skin holds everything in place.

Waiting

Neighborhood birds
searching for refuge
from the coming snowstorm
swoop through the trees
as I pace between window and chair

A huge crow lands
on the porch railing,
cocks his head,
then turns to show off
his dark silhouette

Winter

Morning snowstorm—
the only bird in the bare cherry tree,
a red cardinal

After Snow

A scattering of tiny footprints
on wind-swept snow—
a mourning dove lands
on the crusty ridge,
waddles through the smear of
earth overflow from planters.
Her feet pump the earth.
Wings drawn tight to the wind,
she closes her eyes,
soaking in the chilly afternoon sun

Invitation

Old snow glistens
like warm sand

On the table ginger tea
in a porcelain cup

Winter Moon

Milky stars in a winter sky
        drift above
                a bowl of a moon,
        then drop,
                filling the bowl
                        till it tips,

splashes moonlight on bare trees
        on pebbles along the streambed
                into shallow pools

Winter in Rock Creek Park

Washington, DC

On sunless winter days,
beech trees light up
brown hillsides
with creamy satin leaves,
glimmer early evening
in the dark, quiet forest
until green hums
in the wind,
and leaves let go,
fluttering
light

February

Afternoon quiet, sky gray,
snow falling, confetti—

Sudden commotion, robins coming from all directions
gather for a moment above the tip top
of a pine tree, descend all at once,
like pulling a gown over the head of a girl.

The tree fills with birds pressing
against each other, brown wings pulled tight
as they turn from side to side, red breasts
glistening under wet snow.
The pine dances in a chilly wind.

Robins spiral off,
the tree now bare but for cone ornaments
dangling on branches.

All afternoon robins fly back and forth,
dressing and undressing the pine tree.

Crocus

Yellow and purple crocus
pop up from marshy grass,
unsteady blooms
tipping color into wind

Fog

wafts over the field—
geese descend
pick at brittle grass

Walk in the Woods

In the woods time falls
out on sun rising through trees,
light splashing on rocks shows up
jack-in-the-pulpit, trout lily,
creek sparkles, rushing over flat stones

I become blonde marsh grass,
rocks ringed by spring snow,
raindrops on flat dark leaves,
and a hawk gliding up and down the diagonal,
circling the mountain's south side
where all is brought to light

WITH DEEPEST GRATITUDE TO

My beloved husband and children for their love and support;
Patrice Wilson who catches the nuance in my poems;
Barbara Henning who shows how to bring clarity to my writing;
Wanji Lee for his artistry in making a book from a manuscript;
Ellen MacDonald for the gorgeous artwork and years of friendship;
Ellen Tabak for her exacting eye in proofreading the manuscript;
Susan D'Angelo who lends a fine-tuned ear and perceptive eye;
Connie McKenna for sharing her love of language and lyric;
Chris Kosky and our conversations between poet and bassist;
The Vomen for our many treasured years of friendship;
Many other friends and colleagues along the way.

ABOUT THE AUTHOR

Heather Grant writes of her experiences in and with the natural world in the different regions where she has lived. Bassist Chris Kosky and Heather perform her poems at a variety of venues in the duo Turn of Phrase, conversations between a poet and bassist. Heather lives in Falls Church, Virginia with her jazz drummer husband Web.

Depending on which ideogram is used,
one definition of the Japanese word for nature (*shizen*) is
"supreme goodness."